A Break-Up
Survival Guide

How Women Can Recover
after a Break-Up

NANCY WYLDE

BALBOA
PRESS

A DIVISION OF HAY HOUSE

Balboa Press books may be ordered through booksellers or by contacting:

Balboa Press
A Division of Hay House
1663 Liberty Drive
Bloomington, IN 47403
www.balboapress.com.au
1-(877) 407-4847

ISBN: 978-1-4525-1228-0 (sc)
ISBN: 978-1-4525-1227-3 (e)

Because of the dynamic nature of the Internet, any web addresses or
links contained in this book may have changed since publication and
may no longer be valid. The views expressed in this work are solely those
of the author and do not necessarily reflect the views of the publisher,
and the publisher hereby disclaims any responsibility for them.

The author of this book does not dispense medical advice or prescribe the use
of any technique as a form of treatment for physical, emotional, or medical
problems without the advice of a physician, either directly or indirectly. The
intent of the author is only to offer information of a general nature to help
you in your quest for emotional and spiritual well-being. In the event you use
any of the information in this book for yourself, which is your constitutional
right, the author and the publisher assume no responsibility for your actions.

Any people depicted in stock imagery provided by Thinkstock are models,
and such images are being used for illustrative purposes only.
Certain stock imagery © Thinkstock.

Printed in the United States of America

Balboa Press rev. date: 11/16/2013

Contents

Introduction

It takes two people to make a relationship, and only *one* to end it. It's often assumed that the one who chooses to end a relationship doesn't go through all the same motions, feelings, and experiences as the one who has been dumped.

Whether you chose to walk away or someone said goodbye to you, it is a painful experience, and the feeling that the rug has been pulled out from under your feet or that you've just been pushed off the precipice still remains.

The intense and powerful emotions that we deal with in these first few days, weeks, and months can sometimes be so consuming that we become oblivious to everyone and everything else around us.

Though a grieving process is natural, it is important to maintain our balance, as spiralling downwards can have serious consequences. My first break-up was after a seventeen-year marriage that I chose to end. For me, it was perhaps the most difficult decision to make, but it was a decision based on what was best for both of us.

I could see our future; the writing was on the wall. I would have ended up hating him with a passion, and we would have ended up two strangers under the same roof, with no love for one another—only contempt and disdain. No one should live like that. We are all children of God.

We are all worthy and deserving of happiness, joy, laughter, love, and the wonderful experiences that go with sharing a life with someone we love and respect. Having had no experience in how to deal with my break-up, and having no resources, knowledge, or access to assistance and guidance through such an ordeal, I resorted to medication and alcohol—sometimes at the same time—to subdue and ease my agony. And agonising it was.

At the time of the break-up, I had three very small children, whose lives were dramatically affected, and a husband for whom I did not hold any hatred or contempt. Rather, I felt enough compassion to let him go because I had no choice but to be true to myself. For if I could not be true to myself, I could hardly dispense advice and counsel to anyone else.

This book is the result of some of the things we either fail to do or need to remember to do after a break-up, when we are picking ourselves up off the floor, so to speak. It isn't rocket science, and I certainly will not be able to tell you how to take the pain away, because no one can offer that.

Nevertheless, often we as women find ourselves with more challenges than men because we remain with children to care for while we are in that painful and sometimes desperate state, both emotionally and mentally. Some women also have no work, no career, limited or no income, and no family, resulting in utter helplessness and desolation.

It is my sincerest hope and aim to offer you tips, reminders, and a little advice on what you can do to help yourself get through this difficult time. I'll share ways to cultivate some self-love and become more present, more in the moment, move joyfully forward towards a new you—a better you. You can achieve a new life that you *can* create over time with a little dedication and the willingness to work on yourself.

There is light at the end of the tunnel. Only this I can promise you.

2

It's Over ... The End
of Your World?

The first thing that often happens when we are dealing with what seems to be the end of our world is that our health suffers. We stop eating well, or we eat sporadically. Most times, it is just barely enough to keep us going, such as coffee to keep us awake and moving and junk food, just for the sake of putting something in our mouths. Mostly, this is a result of friends and family saying, "You have to eat." In reality, we want nothing more than to stop eating, stop drinking, and just roll over and die, because it seems that a death has just occurred. And in a sense, it has.

The "death" is our old lives, and it is natural to feel a sense of grief. A big part of us is no longer there. We have invested so much in someone else, and now that is gone.

It is quite healthy to grieve. In fact, I highly recommend it. But do it in a way that is productive.

Productive Grieving? Who Ever Heard of That?

After my first marriage of seventeen years broke down, my father saw that I was not coping emotionally. He came to speak with me one day and took me to a spot on the farm we lived on. He said, "This is a spot I have made for you, a kind of grave if you like, a burial spot where I think you need to come to. Find things of your past that you would like to bury, things that remind you of your past with your former husband. Then dig a hole, bury them, and treat it like a grave. Wear black clothing for a period of time, and mourn if you must, but come here to grieve and then move on."

As he spoke, it was as if my father had offered me the key to moving on. In a way, he did.

I followed his instructions to the letter. I grieved and mourned at appropriate times, but when I walked away from that spot, I stopped grieving and mourning. I went on with what I call "the business of daily living."

My life began to change little by little after that.

Tip: Find a place in your backyard you can call your "memorial ground," if you wish. If you live in an apartment, buy a huge pot with sand in it or fill it with dirt. There you have your little burial ground. Now bury things like his toothbrush, his comb, bits of a shirt you've torn up, or something he's left behind—anything that reminds you of that past life. Visit it every day, and cry if you want. One day you will forget to visit the memorial spot, and then you will know you are on your way to healing!

3

Put Your Health First

Your health is your most valuable asset during this time, because if your physical health goes down the drain, then nearly everything else will follow suit. And by that, I mean your health on a psychological and spiritual level as well.

As you begin to spiral downwards into a bottomless abyss, you will find that it will most definitely affect every area of your life. It serves you nothing to stay in a state of perpetual grief, depression, worry, and utter desperation. All it does is keep you there.

You do not do yourself or anyone else any favours by not eating or by curling up in a ball and wishing to stay there until someone finds you—or until the next Prince Charming comes into your life to give you meaning.

Only *you* can find purpose and meaning for your life. You cannot find your identity, your joy, or your raison d'être in another person. This book is *not* about how to replace the person you just lost with another one ASAP. Because to do that at this point would be nothing short of disastrous!

You will have many well-meaning friends who say the way to heal a broken heart is to find another guy. Really? You are probably in a catatonic state, a total mess right now, good for no one or nothing, and you really think this is a great time to find another relationship? I don't think so.

Tell your well-meaning friends that if they love you, they will help you heal. What you need is to put things into perspective right now, this very minute, before you do anything.

When I suffered my first relationship breakdown, I turned to prescribed medication, and when that didn't work, I turned to alcohol. Though it was I who had ended the relationship, I still suffered through the grieving process that goes with separation. I had lost the life I knew. I was scared and felt as if the earth had opened up and swallowed me. I wasn't sure of anything. Only thirty-four years young and with three young children, I was very uncertain emotionally—and on almost every other level. I had no self-esteem, had no self-confidence, and feared almost everything.

The only way I felt I could cope, at first, was through medication. This is not to say that medication does not have its place. I am of the belief that if one requires prescribed medication, then one should use it. But I did not do well with medication. Without a doubt, the alcohol was destructive. I did not have an addiction problem; it was easy to toss away when I noticed it was the first thing I reached for when things were getting too hard for me. Turning to medication or alcohol or any other form of substance to alleviate emotional pain is *not* productive. I learned the hard way, but I learned. And for that, I am grateful.

Tip A: Don't use medication or alcohol as a way to get through the pain and trauma of separation. It only serves to make you feel less and less in control of your life. The way to healing is not in looking to sources outside of you for relief. And I know only too well of the need for relief of that kind of agonising pain. You've been dumped or you had to end it. The grief can make people insane, but the solution is to get to a place on your own that makes you feel better.

During this time, you may not feel like eating. In fact, you won't want to eat. Your appetite will dwindle considerably, or eating will just make you sick. Avoid eating junk food, though you may not feel like cooking for yourself. I used to hate eating alone, so I wouldn't bother eating, but that was not sensible. The last thing you need is your health to fail you. So make sure you eat well. If you are like me and feel you'd eat better if you had company, make plans so invite a girlfriend or relative to eat with you.

After having had some experience with break-ups, I learned that the only way up was eating to maintain my health. I knew if I had my health, everything else would surely follow in time. And it did.

By the time I got around to my third break-up, I was a real pro! I was lucky enough to live next door to my family, and I'd make sure I would eat with one of my sisters or my parents. Though I didn't eat much, I would ensure I was eating properly and eat in company. It makes a difference. Pay attention, and you'll notice it yourself.

Likewise, be careful about overeating as a way of alleviating stress and anxiety. This can result in unwanted weight gain.

Tip B: Ensure you eat well. Even if you are not hungry, there are ways you can improve that, and it's so easy.

Don't eat junk. Avoid that trap we so often fall into of grabbing a box of chocolates (also known as a girl's best comfort food) and eating the whole box to make yourself feel better. For goodness' sake, you have to eat well. It's no effort to eat fresh fruit, vegetables, and salads with some protein. Keep up with your carbohydrates, the healthy kind that comes from our vegetables like broccoli, carrots, etc. and not from packets of high-sugar cereals, pizza, pasta, and potatoes. Yeah, I love them too, but as I often say to others, "I eat what is good for me, not what I like, and that is the secret to my health and my lean body."

You honestly don't need a tutorial on eating healthy. There is so much information that is readily available to us about how to eat well. All you need to do is look it up on Google!

Tip C: Take up some form of exercise. If you can afford to join an exercise club do so, if not you can purchase a DVD on any form of excise you like, be it Pilates, aerobics, tai chi, kettlenetics and do it from the comfort of your own home. Have a girlfriend or several girlfriends join you if you want to make this fun. Walk a lot, or if you are like me and love gardening, then go into the garden and get in touch with Mother Earth, which is one of the best things you can do for yourself at a time like this.

If you have a dog, you are even luckier. Take your dog for long walks. Don't run; pace yourself. You are not working towards the Marathon Quest, just trying to raise your energy levels. If you don't have a dog and need motivation to get out there and walk, then find a friend who is happy to walk with you. It doesn't have to be every day or even every second day. Only twenty minutes, and I know you can find the time. Remember you're on your own now, and the time your ex took up can be directed into other areas of your life like taking care of *you*.

Tip D: Talk, talk, talk. Now you know we girls are great at talking! Don't shut up. Your girlfriends love to listen. This is what we are made for! Have you forgotten? Your best friend is your girlfriend who is made for this kind of thing.

Don't run to a male friend with your woes, because you are just far too vulnerable right now and all you need to hear are those magic words, "He left you? What an arse! You? Such a beautiful, talented, gorgeous, sexy woman? Was he blind? Did he have eyes? Couldn't he see the treasure trove he just up and left? Why, I should be so lucky to have had you as my girlfriend. I would have known how to treat you right! What a loser he was. How lucky the next guy will be!" And you will be thinking, *Goo, goo, gah, gah. Oh my God, this guy is just so amazing! He sees something in me the other guy didn't. He is so wonderful; he understands me. He is so good for me.* No! Let's not jump right back into another bleeding mess! Take my advice: don't go there, girlfriend. It's a beehive!

Tip E: You want to move forward, right? Then this is important.

Plan your meals ahead of time. Rather than sitting down and playing Roy Orbison's "It's Over" while crying over a lost love, get pen to paper and write a list of the meals you are going to make for yourself over the next week. This will keep you well organised and will not fall into the bad habit of just eating whatever. The key to eating well and eating right is to get organised in this area.

Beauty

<u>Do you look in the mirror?</u> Sometimes we avoid it, because we don't like what we see. We tend not to care too much about the way we look when we're feeling down and depressed about our situation. Quite often, we just throw anything on and avoid doing our hair and make-up or prettying ourselves up because … Well, quite frankly, we have no one to dress up for now, do we? However, this can make us feel even worse.

Start looking in the mirror. What do you like and what don't you like? Wrinkles? Grey hair? Puffy eyes and tired looking? You can change the image in the mirror if you want. Do you want fewer wrinkles, or at least to keep them at bay? Grey hair? Well, you can accept it and get a great style or colour it instead! If you take care of *you*, you will start to like that person staring back in the mirror!

Tip A: Here's what you can start to do. Pamper yourself. Treat yourself well. Have a facial or get a massage, if you can afford it. If you can't, buy some great massage oil or make it up yourself (I do!) and get a girlfriend to treat you to a nice massage. Do this at least once a week. Take long baths with bubble bath or lavender oil. Lavender is relaxing. Put nice music on and just enjoy being good to yourself. Do you nails, colour your hair, get a new look, and do whatever you need to do to look better. When you look better, you start to feel better. Be kind to yourself.

You've got to like what you see in the mirror first. Dress up! You don't have to have a man around to have a reason to dress up and look good. I remember after my first break-up that I went around dressed in tracksuits most of the time. I hardly bothered with the way I looked, until one day I noticed I looked rather tragic! I just didn't care about the way I looked and was starting to dress and look older than my mother! You don't need a fortune to dress in nice clothes or look good. You don't need designer labels either.

You never know who you're going to meet or run into, so dress to impress!

Always!

<u>Are you wearing the right clothes?</u> Sometimes we aren't happy with our bodies, because we are trying to get them to fit in clothes that don't compliment the body shape and size! Wearing clothes that have colourful patterns tend to compliment any figure. Bright colours and no stripes! Wear heels with your jeans; being taller makes you feel thinner! Wear jewellery and other accessories to make you feel good, and they also draw attention away from your trouble spots.

Are your clothes too tight? Have them taken out or get a larger size. It's better to look better in a larger size than look horrible in a smaller size, not to mention not being comfortable! Keep the smaller size for when you lose weight. But don't wear them until you do.

Tip B: You don't have to spend an arm and a leg buying clothes. Take a friend and go to a thrift store. Some clothes there have never been worn!

Check the sales and clearance aisles too.

Dating

<u>Why do you want to date?</u> Are you lonely? Do you want or need to feel a void? Do you want to have fun? Are you looking for the next Mr. Right—or Wrong? Let's check on some things.

First, if you are trying to fill a void and are lonely, you are also vulnerable to attract the wrong kind of man. Keep in mind that you are usually not ready to date if the reason behind it is to soothe the aching heart, make the other person jealous, spite your ex, or fill the emptiness because you can't get past the pain on your own.

If you want to get over the hurt and fill that void, call a friend. Join a new group that likes to do the same things you do. Invite a girlfriend over for dinner or out to a movie, or sleep over at your place or hers.

Next, you need to pamper yourself. Remember what I had mentioned earlier about being kind to you. Date yourself for a while. You need to focus on you! What do you have to offer in a relationship? Are you happy? Can you handle being alone? Do you really like yourself? Do you know yourself? If you answer no to any of these questions, then *you* need to fill that void with *you*. Men are not put on earth to fill our void. Yes, it hurts to be alone now. Give yourself some time. Reflect on inventing *you* and liking *you*.

If you must date (though I strongly recommend a substantial period of time to work on getting yourself together on so many levels before dating), at least do it sensibly. Otherwise, you are going to jump at the first person that strikes your fancy!

Tip A: Don't start looking for Mr. Right. Find out who you are and where you are going, and be happy being single. Then go out and have fun. You will attract Mr. Right. And if you pursue online dating, do it for fun. Go slowly, and be safe.

Online dating—a good idea? Yes and no. What are you looking for? Are you looking for someone to go out with? Do you need someone just to talk to?. Do you feel the need for affection? There have been successes with online dating, and if you are ready to date again, it is worth trying.

Start with just one dating service to see if you like it. It's hard to keep up with them all. If you find you don't like it after a week, then try another. Make sure you stay as anonymous as you can, for as long as you can, and keep your private information like your phone number, email address, and home address secure until you get to know a person via the dating service communication avenues.

Then when you feel like you can go to the next level, give him your IM address and text message. This is a great way to communicate. Inhibitions are down, and you are more likely to ask questions you really want and need to ask. This will help with your screening process. After this, move to email, to phone, and then a meeting. When you do meet, meet in a public place. Old-fashioned rules apply here. Don't bring him home or to the kids yet! You still need to get to know him before you start intimacy or introduce him to the kids.

Tip B: Date a few guys this way. Don't just screen one out. You need to wait until a few have made it this far before you go to the next level.

You are going on your first date! Come prepared, be safe, and be confident! OK, be prepared—what do you mean? Well, what if it doesn't go so well? Have a backup plan. First, make sure you meet him somewhere or go with friends on a double date if the situation is attainable. Do not have him pick you up. That way, it is not uncomfortable having him take you home or needing to contact someone else to come get you. Have a phone ready in case you need the backup advice of a friend. At this point, you should be ready to date and be happy with who you are!

Tip C: Conversations should not be about the problems you have had with your past relationships. If he asks, tell him that it wasn't to be and now you have a better understanding of where you are in your life and what you want out of it. Keep the conversation positive, and if you are uncomfortable with a question, be vague and then ask him a question. Guys like to talk about what they like to do.

Blind dates. I have had limited experience personally on blind dates. Fact is, I had one blind date my entire life, and it was nothing short of a disaster. It put me off forever!

I had been under the assumption I was having a coffee with an old acquaintance I had not seen in about twenty years. A friend of mine set it up for me. I really had no reason to believe it was going to be anything more than a coffee with an old friend and perhaps later turn into someone to talk to or go to dinner with from time to time. I was a little apprehensive at first, but we talked on the phone once and seemed to click. Given that we knew each other from the past, all seemed fine.

I played it safe. I met him at a café and drove myself so that I was in control of when I wanted to leave. What I wasn't ready for was what came out of his mouth after thirty minutes talking about what we had been doing the past twenty years or so.

He leaned over and said, "Well, I'm in!"

"In for what?" I asked.

"This relationship thing. I'll tell you now that I'm not into the romance rubbish. I like to get straight to the point, no messing about. And I like what I see, so let's get on with the dating business."

At that point, I was actually lost for words. I excused myself and went to the ladies room. I phoned my sister. I was panic stricken, literally. I didn't know what to do. I didn't want to run off, because he was a friend of a friend of mine. I knew I wasn't going to be in any harm, but this man clearly had the wrong idea, and I had to find a way to let him down without being rude and abrupt.

On returning from the ladies room, I smiled and told him I was still going through somewhat of a difficult time getting over the last relationship and that I wasn't in any place emotionally or mentally to move towards another relationship, as it would be a disaster.

I couldn't wait to get home, and it was the first and last blind date I ever went on. Personally, I don't recommend them.

Tip D: Even if you think you know someone or it is a person recommended by a friend, don't go out until you have had several conversations with him. With Facebook, email, phone, and texting these days, you have ample opportunity to get to know where a man is at and a bit about him before you meet up with him. Having some knowledge about the kind of person he is and what he is looking for can save you some embarrassing moments.

Transitioning

So you are now in the midst of a major life change. All life changes, although frequently painful, can be unexpected instruments for growth and progress. You now face a unique time to evaluate many things in your life and how they relate to your personal happiness.

Maybe your husband or significant other has decided to move on, or perhaps you jointly have decided that this is the best action to take for many reasons. There are major job changes on the horizon. Now what? How do you survive this major life change?

Here are eight survival tips to help you through these kinds of situations.

Tip 1: First of all, don't do anything in a hurry. Wait until you've talked about your feelings and reactions with a trusted friend, a coach, or an objective listener. Don't rush into dating if your relationship has ended or into the job market if you have been laid off. Avoid making mistakes at a time when good judgement may be clouded by feelings of anger, denial, or depression. Such a critical transition first requires a period of reflection as well as a logical approach.

Tip 2: Acknowledge, honour, process, and deal with the emotions tied to finding yourself in this place and situation. Denying your emotions only delays your progress. Know that it is normal to experience a variety of feelings. While change can occur very quickly, our transition and adjustment to the change are very personal and take time.

Tip 3: Find a trusted friend, counsellor, member of the clergy, family member, or professional with whom you feel totally safe, and ask if he or she is willing to let you vent without judgement. Allow yourself to vent safely with this person. This will enable you to move more quickly through the rebounding process. Once your emotions are processed, you will find the energy to immerse yourself in the activities to move forward.

Tip 4: Accept the support of others. Let you family members and close friends know what you're experiencing and, most importantly, how they can assist you. Relying on others' support can create a team effort and a positive working environment for you. You most likely would be happy to help your family and colleagues if they were in such a transition, so allow them to do the same for you now.

Tip 5: Take charge of the unexpected. It may be that you did not see this coming at all, even though in hindsight there may have been warning signals that were either discarded or not dealt with. Decide that you are in charge of your destiny, and take the necessary actions to rebound.

Tip 6: Take care of yourself physically (get enough sleep, drink plenty of water, eat well, etc.) so that you have the energy to do what you need to do.

Tip 7: Take action. The way to rebound from this setback is to take action. Figure out what you need to do now to take care of yourself, your children, and your finances, and start doing those things. Know that you *can* take charge of your current situation and move forward towards what you truly want in your life.

Tip 8: Maintain perspective and a positive mental attitude towards yourself, your family, your friends, and your situation in general. This is the single most important ingredient to moving forward successfully. To ensure a successful transition, stay mentally alert, physically strong, and socially connected. Realise that this is a process, and pace yourself accordingly.

As is the case in many of the sudden, unexpected events you may have faced in your life, you are now at a decision point. Will you consider the situation a problem or an opportunity? Choose opportunity, seek the assistance you need, and move forward with grace and ease.

Career

Since so much change is happening in your personal life, this can have an impact on your performance at work. Even though employers can be sympathetic, they still have a business to run, and your productivity can be substantially diminished during this time.

You need your job! It's the last thing you need to lose right now. Stay focused on your job when you're at work. If you don't want co-workers or colleagues to know what's going on in your personal life, then at the very least have a private meeting with your employer.

Let your employer know of your circumstances so that he or she can cut you some slack. If you need time off to sort things through emotionally, then ask for it rather than turn up to work unhappy and distressed all the time. Many workplaces offer free counselling. If your workplace has this option, then by all means, take it!

Tip A: Stay positive and open minded about the work situation. No one wants a whiner or complainer on their team or staff. Regardless of how you may feel about what is happening, look on the bright side and stay focused on being thankful for all you have, including your job. If it weren't for the job challenges, you wouldn't have a job, right?

Tip B: Take on more responsibility. Be prepared to lend a hand and take initiative every day. Yes, every time you raise your hand or take on something new, think of it as showing your boss that you are an enthusiastic, valuable player on the team.

Tip C: Talk to your employer about your situation. Take time off, if you can. Employers are human too. They understand how unexpected and traumatic changes in our lives can affect our work performance.

Tip D: Take counselling if it is offered. Your employer will see this as a genuine attempt on your part to help yourself through this.

The Law of Attraction and the Attitude of Gratitude

The law of attraction succinctly put it that "like attracts like." We attract what we think. For example, the people in our lives, the money in our bank accounts, the house we live in, the furniture in our house, the stuff we have, the job we have, our work colleagues, the man we have or don't have in our life, and our friends are attracted into our lives through our thoughts and feelings. So if you are in a state of lack, you continue to attract that lack. If you are anxious, distressed, and depressed, you will continue to attract these conditions that cause you to remain in such an emotional state. When you focus or give your attention to what you don't have or what is missing in your life, you continue to get more of the same stuff showing up in your life.

Tip A: Create a list. Start to think about what you *do* have. You can do this constructively by writing it down on paper or a notebook where you can add to it every day.

Begin by writing down the things that you have in front of you immediately. For example, the dwelling you live in (be it humble), the clothes you have, the shoes on your feet, the blankets you have in winter, the food on the table, the electricity, the cold and hot running water, your children, your job, your car, your friends, your relatives, your bed, your health, and your life. You see what I mean?

As you begin to make this list, you will notice that each day you will continue to add to it, and instead of thinking about what you *don't* have, you start to shift your thinking towards what you *do* have. You will notice that you will begin writing down some of the simplest things you've taken for granted!

Eliminate negative thoughts. Are you thinking negatively? Do you continually go over what has gone wrong in your life? Do you think about what you should have done instead?

These are the thoughts that, by continually reliving them day in and day out, whether you think them or talk about them, continue to appear in your life.

Tip B: Start becoming an observer of your thoughts. When you start to think of a negative experience, deliberately choose a better and more positive thought. Avoid engaging in negative conversations, and choose to talk about what new experiences you want realised in your life.

Use positive affirmations as a way of replacing the negative self-talk.

Develop an attitude of gratitude. Have nothing to be grateful for? Check your pulse! In learning to attract more of what you *do* want in your life and less of what you *don't*; develop an attitude of being grateful for absolutely everything that comes your way. Be grateful for a rainy day as much as you would be grateful for the sunshine. Be an appreciator of everything that is already in your life and everything that begins to show up.

Try to see the glass as half-full as opposed to viewing it half-empty. In doing this, you will begin to attract more of what you *do* have!

Tip C: When you wake up each morning in bed, nominate all the things you have to be grateful for. For example, I am grateful for a wonderful night's sleep. I am grateful for my warm, cosy bed; my warm, cosy dressing robe; my slippers that I can slip my feet into; my hot shower; my coffee; my breakfast; my clean and freshly ironed clothes; my two legs I walk on; my eyesight; my hearing; and my sense of taste. The list will be endless.

As you start to do this, it may seem odd because you are so used to taking things like vision, hearing, taste, smell, and touch for granted. It is a gift! Be grateful!

Break the habit of attracting negative situations in your life. Instead of focusing on your low-paying job, poor health, unhealthy relationship, or lack of a relationship, focus on breaking the habit of attracting these negatives in your life like any other old bad habit. This will take some effort, especially because negative language and thoughts have been so much a part of your life for years. Replace it with positives! Don't dwell on the negative experiences; they were yesterday. Think about what positive situations you want to draw into your life.

Tip A: Get a scrapbook. Fill the pages with pictures from magazines that depict what you want to see realised in your life, where you want to be, and the kind of happy, fulfilled person you want to become. Make this a work of art, and do this thoughtfully, not willy-nilly. Create as many pages as you want. After all, it's *your* book! Call it your wish book, manifestation book, dream book, or vision book. Make a conscious effort to be specific, and if pictures won't do, then write down what you would like to see realised in your life. Be specific! The universe loves specifics. The more the better! Dare to dream!

Use the law of attraction to reduce stress. Positive affirmations are a great way to reprogram your negative thinking to positive thinking. Think about what you want to create in your life or where you would like to see yourself go. Figure out what you want first. Take an idea about what you want to see realised in your life and repeat it out loud so that it becomes a part of your thinking. Replacing the negative self-talk with positive self-talk will aid in reducing stress.

Tip B: Write up some very simple statements first. Remember you can make as many positive statements as you like! As well, write what you want, not what you don't want. The LOA works like this: It attracts what you give your attention to. Thus, if you say to yourself, "I don't want more of this disaster," then you will end up with more served up to you! If you want more peace and calm in your life, then say, "I am more and more at peace every day."

Repeat your affirmations throughout the day whenever you get the chance. There is no specific amount of times you need to say your affirmations. However, the more times you do it, the better. And anytime of the day you remember is just fine! To help you remember, put your affirmations on Post-It notes in designated places around the house—even in the car!

Tools to Bring You Back into Balance

In one of my books, 7 Steps to Reclaiming Your Personal Power, I discuss various modalities that can be used to bring you back into alignment, to a place of balance. These tools aid you in getting back that *personal power*, as I term it, that we can lose at such critical times of stress and distress in our lives.

In the book, I discuss each of the modalities at length and in some detail, so I will touch on each of them here just briefly. To get more information, please avail yourself of this wonderful little title.

Meditation

Meditation is a key tool in developing personal growth. To grow effectively, we need to find clarity of purpose, and this can be achieved through meditation.

To exactly find a point in the history of mankind where meditation began would be difficult. Suffice to say, it would have commenced many millennia ago. However, what we do know is that meditation began in ancient civilisations.

Many Hindi scholars from India wrote about meditation, and these are better known as the Vedas and the Yoga Sutras, which were written by Patanzali. And then of course there was the meditation of Siddhartha Gautama (Buddha). The East has practised meditation for countless centuries, and though the Western world caught on, it really wasn't until the mid-twentieth century that meditation began to be so popular.

To this day, meditation is still the greatest method to achieving inner peace and well-being and is being recommended by many health practitioners, both in the alternative fields as well as in the orthodox such as general practitioners and specialists. In fact, doctors recommend meditation techniques for many reasons:

- Lower high blood pressure
- lessen anxiety
- Lift depression
- prevent heart failure
- Stop substance abuse
- decrease health-care expenditures
- alleviate ADHD
- Balance metabolic syndrome

- improve overall health
- promote longevity

And these are just a few!

Fifteen minutes of meditation daily can assist with the following and so much more.

- helps you to relax quickly
- improves concentration and clarity of mind
- reduces anxiety and stress
- helps you gain a general sense of well-being
- assists in restoring health
- raises tolerance levels
- increases creativity
- brings out the inherently *content and happy person* from within
- helps to create within you an inner peace and happiness
- assists in both mind and body healing

Through regular meditation, you begin to still the mind, and you build your energy level, self-discipline, and self-control. You will emanate a calm that resonates from within and affects the people with whom you interact in a positive way. You feel balanced. Things unfold naturally and effortlessly. Through these daily quiet periods you set aside for yourself, you can tap into the higher power that lies within you. This power will guide you, inspire you, and help you see new, creative ideas.

Meditation can be practiced in various ways. While there are a number of different meditation techniques, a commonality runs through almost all of them.

If you are new to meditation, you can find a brief explanation on the different ways you can meditate effectively and how to choose the technique that is right for you at the end of this title in resources.

EFT

Emotional freedom technique (EFT) is a universal aid to healing that is changing the way we perceive emotional and physical dysfunction and disease. It allows insight into what really limits our physical and emotional health and well-being.

EFT is a form of *psychological acupressure,* without using needles, of course. The approach is to tap on various body locations while repeating self-accepting statements at different points several times. It is through this tapping that the energy meridians that have become disrupted from our experiences or negative thoughts become more balanced. Of course, the memories of such experiences are never eradicated. But it is the emotional charge that dissolves. The result is lasting, and coupled with that is the positive changes in your thinking.

EFT has been successfully applied to treat a wide range of emotional problems, including anxiety, fears, phobias, trauma, PTSD (post-traumatic stress disorder), guilt, anger, grief, and addictions.

EFT can assist in reducing the emotional upsets towards others, including our partners in our relationships. Couples using EFT can overcome many of the barriers that confront relationships.

Of all the tools I've used to assist me in situations where I felt stuck on or powerless in, EFT has been by far one of the most effective.

While EFT has achieved amazing results with many emotional and physical conditions, it is not intended to replace appropriate medical care and should always be used in conjunction with medical consultation for such conditions that require it.

Solfeggio Frequencies

The solfeggio frequencies come from an ancient musical scale that was thought to be lost centuries ago and was replaced with the scale that is used today (twelve-tone equal temperament with A=440). They are the original sound frequencies used in ancient Gregorian chants; including the great hymn to St. John the Baptist. Many secrets lie within the solfeggio frequencies. Solfeggio frequencies are believed to have the capacity to effect matter and consciousness.

It is an effective way to heal and soothe the body, as well as to achieve a higher state of consciousness. What is astounding about exposing yourself to these frequencies on a regular basis is that they can make big changes in a relatively short time.

The following are the six solfeggio frequencies are:

1. UT 396 Hz—liberating guilt and fear
2. RE 417 Hz—undoing situations and facilitating change
3. MI 528 Hz—transformation and miracles (DNA repair)
4. FA 639 Hz—connecting/relationships
5. SOL 741 Hz—awakening intuition
6. LA 852 Hz—returning to spiritual order

By tapping into one or more of the above modalities on a regular basis, you'll begin to notice that you cope with the changes around you and do so constructively rather than destructively.

A lot is happening to you, and you need your wits about you if you are to move forward. There is nothing outside of yourself that solves your problems, changes your current circumstances, or fixes them! This is why resigning yourself to what it is and finding balance within will help you regain a sense of control over matters.

Whenever you find yourself reminiscing about the past events or the life you had with your ex, it will only serve to keep you in the past; moving forward will be hindered. This doesn't mean you shouldn't think about it. Of course, when wounds are fresh, it is *all* you think about. But if you can get into a habit of practising meditation, listening to the solfeggio frequency of your choice, or using emotional freedom technique just for fifteen minutes a day, you will become more present, more in the moment, rather than remaining in the past.

10

Parenting

When you are first divorced or if you've just separated, your children will ask a lot of questions. You need to be careful of what you say. First and foremost, you need to make sure that they understand it is not their fault in any way and this is about grown-up choices only. You don't need to go into detail in the beginning.

They need to understand just the basics without putting their father down and without you taking the blame to try to protect the children. Answer one question at a time, with one simple answer, using the gentle truths. As they get older and want to know more, then you can express more detail in an age-appropriate manner. And again, be careful not to call names, place blame, or be disrespectful to the child's father or to yourself.

Tip A: Listen to your children's questions. Reassure them. Tell them that is a good question and you will think about it, and then answer them after some thought.

Let the children know exactly when they can expect answers from you. Basically, when they ask questions, you can always answer, "This is a tough time for each of us for different reasons. Your dad and I love you very much, and that's the most important thing for you to know. This is about grown-up things, so let's work to help you not worry about those things. Let's focus on things we can do to feel happy instead of sad. Let's take things one step at a time, and I will answer your questions the very best I can. Again, remember that we both love you very much and this is about grown-up stuff and not you. You have done nothing wrong at all."

At this point when you are emotional, you need to carefully select your words. It's important for you to seek guidance for the tough questions you *will* be asked and learn to answer with an age-appropriate response that will empower you and your children and your circumstance. Each divorce is different, but all children experience very similar feelings during divorce, regardless of the specifics. If you cannot afford a therapist, practice with a friend you trust how you will tell your children and what you will say. And anticipate the possible questions they can ask so you are prepared. Make sure this person you speak with is a positive role model for you. *Your* reactions to crisis will teach your children how to react in crisis.

Tip B: Encourage children to see the good in their father and you. Share a story with them about how excited you were to bring them in to this world with their father when they were born. Compliment qualities they have of their father that you admire, and tell them that even though the two of you are going through some grown-up problems, you will support a loving relationship with both parents. For instance, if they have their father's eyes, you could mention, "You have your father's kind, brown eyes" or "You are funny just like your dad, and that's a great quality to have."

This will be difficult, especially if there has been abuse. Work to not allow your children to do the time for something they had nothing to do with. Continue to remind them that you and their father are dealing with the grown-up stuff and you both love them no matter what the grown-ups choose.

Tip C: Don't tell the children about qualities they have that you didn't like about their father. This will only make them question how much you love them, especially if they have been told how much they look like the father. One adult child of divorce mentioned how she purposely made herself sick on picture day at school because when she was fifteen her mother told her she looked just like her father, and that's why there were very few photos of her in the home. From that point, that fifteen-year-old girl spent her life truly believing she was ugly, because of the anger her mother had towards her father and that one little statement the mother made. This fifteen-year-old girl spent her life trying to be perfect, going through one abusive relationship after another while trying to get someone, anyone, to help her believe she was pretty enough. Don't let this be your child.

How do I create and agree to solid boundaries?

It is important to set defined boundaries regarding your ex/potential ex and his access to you, your home, and other previously shared situations and environments, including shared friendships. Keep communication simple, to the fact, and as minimum as possible. Social activities should be treated as businesslike as possible. If you are not yet capable of doing this, divide the activities, and do not attend them together. Your animosity *will* be apparent to the children. You are not together anymore, so you should conduct yourself as though the other is off limits to any affection, personal access, or emotional confrontations—*especially in front of your children*. This includes phone calls.

Visitation—If you have school-aged children, it is always best for the children if you can make exchanges at day-care or school. You drop them off at school, for example, and your ex picks them up from school. It's emotionally stressful on children of any age to be forced to leave one parent to go to the other. (More on this later.)

Tip D: Agree to a positive communication style. For example, tell him that you expect he will not visit your home unannounced and you will do the same. Make all visitation arrangements or discussions about the children through email or phone while the children are at school. This can easily be accomplished during your daytime work hours. This is *always* in the best interest of the children and less stressful to them.

Parent Power for You and Your Children

Teaching children respect is of utmost importance. It's never too late, and (as most of us know) it's much easier to teach this right from the start. But if this has not been the case, then start now. It is much easier for your children to trust you and your ex when they see you react with respect for yourself and your ex. It's not the situation that will hurt or help your children the most; it's how you react to crisis—crisis of any kind. It's the old adage "Practice what you preach." *Show* your children that you can see the positive side of things, even though they can be painful. React with kindness and understanding of your own feelings, and they will learn to do the same.

Tip E: Model positive reactive behaviours while reinforcing those behaviours with words. Young children need your good manners and respectful words in order to learn the same. Older children need to *see and hear* what you are teaching them about respect.

The most important advice I can give is that feelings are factual to the person experiencing the feelings. Never give a response to your children, such as "Suck it up," "You will be fine," or "Just deal with it." Give them words and ways to cope with the break-up. When your children (of any age) tell you they are mad or hurt, you simply say, "I understand why you must be feeling this way, and I am sorry. What can we do together to help you through this?" Then find fun and genuine ways to show them it's OK to be sad and that you will get through this *together*.

I was once told, "You have to feel it to heal it." Remember this phrase when your children are angry or sad about your grown-up choices they had nothing to do with. They feel powerless. Your reactions, words, and love can help them feel powerful and loved.

Summary

On Health

- Take care of your health.
- Eat plenty of colourful fruits and vegetables.
- Avoid sugary, highly processed, refined foods.
- Avoid stocking sweets in the house.
- Make time to exercise, or at least walk!
- If you are not at your healthy weight, change a few things to help you feel better.

On Beauty

- If you don't like what you see in the mirror, you can change that image.
- You need to like the person in the mirror.
- Take care of your skin and hair with some simple tips.
- Wear sunscreen with your moisturiser.

- Take time out to dress well just for *you!*
- Walk, rest, and most importantly, sleep!
- Make sure your clothes compliment your body shape and size!
- You don't need a lot of money to look good. Go to a thrift store to save on clothes.

On Dating

- Don't start looking for Mr. Right too soon.
- First, find out who *you* are and where you are going.
- Be happy being single; learn to love *your* company first.
- Learn to pamper yourself.
- Date yourself for a while.
- Have fun with your girlfriends.
- When you want to start dating again, take some sensible precautions.

On Transitioning

- Do nothing in a hurry, especially when you are feeling lonely.
- Acknowledge, honour, process, and deal with your emotions.
- Accept the support of others.
- Take charge of the unexpected.

- Take care of yourself physically.
- Know that you can take charge of your current situation and move forward.
- Maintain a perspective and a positive mental attitude.

On Career

- Stay positive and open-minded about the work situation.
- You have to protect your job, as your family is counting on you.
- Be grateful that you have a job.
- Be prepared to lend a hand in the workplace.
- Take initiative.
- Take risks at work that others may not take.
- Demonstrate that you are an enthusiastic, valuable player on the team.

On Law of Attraction and the Attitude of Gratitude

- Create a list of all the things you *do* have.
- Eliminate negative thoughts, and become an observer of your thoughts.
- Use positive affirmations to establish a way of replacing the negative self-talk.

- Develop an attitude of gratitude. Be an appreciator of things you already have.
- Break the habit of attracting negatives by focusing on positives.
- Buy a scrapbook and fill it with pictures of what you want to see realised in your life.
- Use LOA to reduce stress by using affirmations.

On Tools to Bring You Back into Balance

- Remember you can't do this alone. And you don't have to.
- Choose a tool that suits you.
- Find fifteen minutes a day for yourself to bring your stress levels down.
- Be consistent, and you will notice how much better you cope.

On Parenting

- Make sure the children understand that they are not at fault for the choices grown-ups make.
- Listen to your children.
- Do not be disrespectful to the children's father or to yourself.
- Reassure them that they are loved.
- Encourage your children to see the good in their father and you.

- Define set boundaries regarding your ex or potential ex and his access to you.
- Keep communication simple.
- Agree to a positive communication style.
- Teach your children respect.
- Model positive reactive behaviour.

12

Something to Think About

I do believe that much of what we continually attract in our lives, especially one relationship after another, is a reflection of what is going on inside of us. This was the harshest realisation I ever had to face when it came to the end of my own personal relationships.

There is no power in blaming the other person as not being "the right one" or that there was something the other person did or was. Ask yourself, "What is it in me that continues to attract the same kind of situation or person into my life over and over and over again?"

Much of my conditioning and watching what my mother and her generation settled for was so ingrained in my psyche that I took it on-board without realising it. I watched as my mother's and grandmother's generations settled for less than adequate. I came from a conditioning that went something like this:

"You should be so lucky he even looks at you and that he lets you breathe the same oxygen as he does." Never in any of the relationships I experienced in the earlier part of my life did I feel adequate, worthy, and deserving.

It was my lack of self-respect and self-love and my worthlessness that continued to attract the same kind of man into my life, over and over again. I kept attracting men who thought as little of me as I thought of myself. I could not blame any one of them for treating me any less than they did, because I had not learned to love myself first. So how could they give me the love and respect that I did not have for myself?

Very recently, I was given something from a friend that was truly awe-inspiring and came to me when I had made one of the most difficult decisions of my life. And I did it because I had grown to love myself. I finally developed the self-respect and self-love I so deserved. I would like to share this with you, and I hope that you remember that this journey you call your break-up is a corner you are turning. It is happening because it is supposed to happen. If it didn't, you would not want to improve yourself, your life, and your circumstances. If it did not happen, you would not strive to better yourself and search for answers. You would not go out and seek more. God is wonderful, God is great, and God is magnificent. God knows the desires of your heart.

Respect yourself enough to walk away from anything that no longer serves you, grows you, or makes you happy. If you aren't being treated with love and respect, check your price tag. Maybe you've marked yourself down. It's *you* who tells people what your worth is. Get off the clearance rack and get behind the glass, where they keep the valuables.

—Greg Bradden. New York Times Bestselling Author of FRACTAL TIME, THE GOD CODE and THE DIVINE MATRIX

13

More on Nancy Wylde

Email me at <u>nancywylde@yahoo.com</u>

You can also find me on Facebook at:
<u>nancy.wylde.3@facebook.com</u>

Website: <u>www.NancyWylde.org</u>

More books by Nancy Wylde

- *Ticket to Freedom: A Self-Empowerment Guide for Women*
- *7 Steps to Reclaiming Your Personal Power*

14

Resources

More on meditation techniques
www.yourbestmeditation.com

More on the Law of Attraction
www.abraham-hicks.com

Emotional Freedom Technique
www.fastereft.com.au
www.bradyates.net

**Solfeggio Frequencies (free
samples and downloads)**
www.mindpowermp3.com

www.ingramcontent.com/pod-product-compliance
Lightning Source LLC
Chambersburg PA
CBHW071244280526
45788CB00004B/1572